ENGAGED

ATHLETICS

How to Leverage the Power of Youth and High School Sports to Impact Overall Student Success

How to leverage the impact of overall
student experience / success?

How do we close the opportunity
gap for all student-athletes?

ENGAGED ATHLETICS

How to Leverage the Power of Youth and High School Sports to Impact Overall Student Success

By

JASON L. PARKER, JD

Happy Self Publishing.

CONTENT

To my lovely partner, best friend and wife Mia Nashay, I love you and thank you for your support. To Jace and Sydney, Daddy loves you. This is for you!

INTRO

I'm well into my first semester at law school when I realize I need a 2.0-grade point average (GPA) to stay in school. As I quickly did the math to calculate my expected GPA for the semester, my forehead starts to sweat and stomach starts to turn! The numbers did not look promising and if they did not change fast, I faced being kicked out of law school!

Part of the problem was that I never wanted to be in law school in the first place. In my heart, I was still playing professional basketball in some of the top leagues in Europe and America. However, after a torn ACL (anterior cruciate ligament) and fractured kneecap in consecutive years; my otherwise successful pro-playing career came to a devastating end.

The swift and unexpected end led to a loss of identity that brought about depression (I call it PTSD--Post-Traumatic Sports Disorder!).

It was during this confusing time that I made the awesome decision to attend law school in the first place. Smart, right? Only the decision turned out to be less like *awesome* and more like *awful*. I was immediately disoriented by the Socratic method, the vernacular, and the pedagogy, and I still don't know what those words mean!

What was clear was the fact that my family was depending on this opportunity. Without any real work experience, relevant connections, or on-point education, this was our chance at a new career and life. I knew I had to figure out a way to succeed despite the circumstances.

What was ironic was that I had always been an excellent student prior to this point. In fact, I had graduated third in my high school class with a 4.6 GPA and followed that up by finishing my freshman year in college with the highest GPA amongst all student-athletes in the Western Athletic Conference (WAC)—(I promise the competition were smarter than the name sounds!)—eventually graduating with high honors. With my previous scholastic success, the answer to my current academic struggles did not make much sense.

However, my previous academic exploits were only surpassed by my athletic accomplishments. As my high school's all-time leading scorer, and one of the top players in Oklahoma, I went on to the University of Tulsa where I led my team in scoring, assists, and steals for two consecutive years. I completed my career as a two-time All-Conference and Academic All-American. I also led my team to two NCAA tournaments culminating in being honored as the National Student-Athlete of the Year Finalist!

But it was not the classroom experiences which stuck with me, rather it was the athletic ones. I could still recall and even taste the 5 a.m. workouts, the pangs of knee surgery, and the thrill of the NCAA tournament crowds. Those transformational experiences were impactful to me, each of them making a lasting imprint in my thoughts, words, and behaviors.

It suddenly dawned on me that the athletics had led to the academics. In other words, the person I was becoming on the court, was the person I continued to be in the classroom. The work ethic, commitment, excellence and drive to succeed that helped me be the best basketball player I could be, had transformed me into the best person I could be.

With this epiphany, I re-subscribed to athletics as the driving force in my life. Every morning at 6 a.m. you could catch me running wind sprints, jumping rope, performing dribbling drills, and lifting weights before my law classes. Most of my classmates thought I was a nut! But just two years later, I graduated law school with honors and passed the Oklahoma Bar Exam!

This experience taught me two things, One: I did not want to be a lawyer! Two: Athletics is a powerful tool that changes lives! When my pro career ended, I mistakenly believed I had lost what made me special. However, basketball helped me form personal character and habits that could be used for the rest of my life; which truly made me special. In essence, I had discovered my super power!

DEVELOPING STUDENTS' SUPERPOWERS

Superpowers are talents deposited in us at birth which are developed through experience. Large amounts of focus and commitment are required to properly develop Superpowers. Think of Spider-Man. Although he was naturally gifted, he could not wield his webbing, wall-climbing, and jumping ability without lots of practice. Even Batman, who is not viewed as naturally gifted, honed his super-powers over time.

Both scenarios demonstrate that devotion to development produces a skill set that most people do not have. Personally, athletics produced a strong work ethic, ability to succeed under pressure, and an unquenchable desire to achieve within me. Those traits have been powerful in every area of my life.

Leverage the force of athletics to help Students develop their Superpowers! Your commitment will lead to life-changing results!

I realized athletics was an outstanding tool that can be used to mold young people to become their very best. When used correctly, sports change lives in ways both small and large. No matter the duration of the playing career, those that buy in are equipped with a skillset unlike that of their peers.

I now have a responsibility to change lives through sport. For many youth today, sports are their only form of true motivation and development. Without it, they often have no sense of real purpose or positivity. Inspiring students, schools, and stakeholders (School/Club Coaches, Teachers/Trainers, & Administrators) to take advantage of this golden opportunity to transform kids into leaders is now my life's passion.

I have been blessed to have my high school uniform retired, been named a collegiate All-American, been paid to travel the world as a professional athlete, and have earned a law degree. Yet those accomplishments pale in comparison to changing lives as a committed educator and Youth Sports consultant.

I now offer this information to students and schools knowing that it is the key to unlocking student's greatest strengths. How do I know? Because I'm not just a proponent of this methodology, I'm a product of it.

CHAPTER 1

CHARACTER, CONNECTIONS, COLLEGE

From grade school to high school many people, worldwide, have participated in athletic programs at some point in their life. In fact, most reading this book have had their own unique experiences with sports. Those adults who spent extended periods of time involved in youth sports have likely had their life shaped by athletics in a profound way (perhaps good or bad). Whether you recognize it or not, those experiences have played a key role in the person you are today.

ATHLETICS & ACTIVITIES

While the focus of this book is based on athletics, I truly believe the same transformational takeaways are available in other activities as well. As an educator, I regularly see how Band, One-Act Plays, Dance, JROTC, Speech & Debate, Robotics Club, Bowling Club, Archery, and others are being used to truly engage and bring the best out of youth today.

Whenever I use the term athletics, know that it is interchangeable with all activities that engage students.

Likely your character, connections, or college experience was shaped by athletics. These key attributes have lasting implications throughout the course of our adult lives. How does athletics shape our character? Perhaps you developed an exceptional work ethic, ability to persevere through difficulties, or work well with others.

How has athletics impacted our connections? Sports interactions, whether we are patronizing or participating, can serve as the source of some of our most impactful relationships. Lastly, how has athletics impacted our college experiences? Maybe you received athletic aid or some of your best college experiences were as a fan of a sports program. Athletics often plays a pivotal role in which schools we choose to attend.

Our sports experiences from grade school through high school leave us with preconceived notions about how we should use sports to shape students. However, athletics is fueled by competition and emotion (generally good things) which often cause us to lose focus of the bigger picture. As a result, most parents, coaches, and schools are not using sport correctly.

I know because I was among this group. As a former high school All-Stater, Division I All-American and Professional Athlete, I assumed I possessed the knowledge to provide my son the skills he needed to thrive athletically. However, the opposite was the case. I rode him, demeaned him, and pushed him past his limits too soon. Instead of thriving through athletics; he was terrified by it.

Then I sat back, reevaluated what was most important and designed a system that would keep us both on the right path.

As a result, Engaged Athletics was born! Engaged Athletics mission is to change kids' lives from the INSIDE OUT, using sport as a tool. We

3

want to provide the information, motivation, and inspiration that leads students, schools, and stakeholders to realize the power of sport and use it correctly. This book serves as the first step in this mission. I hope you will join me in creating Engaged Athletes worldwide!

CHAPTER 2

THE POWER OF SPORTS

Sports drive our culture today. From the playtime preference of small kids to an adult obsession; sports are extremely impactful in our world. Billion-dollar sports networks, professional franchises and apparel giants demonstrate our enchantment with sports. However, these behemoth industries and organizations all rest on the foundation of amateur athletics (from pre-K to high school). In essence, youth sports make college and professional sports possible!

Sport-loving adults often create sport-loving children. Those children grow up seeing large crowds cheering on athletes and attentive to their every move. Over time, kids too become engrossed in athletics and begin to hold athletes in high regard. As a result, it is kids and their parents who largely consume sports entertainment, purchase sports apparel and drive ticket sales of colleges and professional franchises. So let's stop and think, in this equation, who really has the power?

Wouldn't it be interesting if parents, coaches and schools took hold of this power to create better young people?

REALIZE VALUE OF ATHLETIC EDUCATION

I define educators as those paid to design programs that educate kids. The list includes School Administrators, Teachers, School Coaches, Club Coaches, and Sport/Performance Trainers, to name a few. These groups all play a role in developing students. However, a mindset shift has to occur. Educators must first realize the value of athletic education. Secondly, they must act to leverage this power to change students, schools and the stakeholders that surround them.

Athletics and activities are viewed by educators as extra-curricular activities. Consequently, sports have become an 'extra' component of education rather than an integral one. This mindset establishes athletics as last on the educational totem pole. (What would you think if your boss gave you an extra task or responsibility beyond your already maxed out priority list)?

However, as demonstrated above, sports can provide educators with an awesome educational tool. What if we began to make athletics a priority in our Schools today?

Schools have trouble engaging students with normal educational content. This is not the case when it comes to sports. To the contrary, many students exhibit intense focus anytime athletics comes into play. We can use this attention to drive student's motivation in other important areas.

Athletics is the greatest tool available for educators to inspire students to become better at anything. Whether it's becoming a better batter, swimmer, teammate, or mathematician; helping students strive toward positive goals creates a habit of excellence within them.

Educators must act to leverage this great tool to change entire schools. Successful athletic programs and athletes garner tons of attention inside the school and out. This enables student-athletes to embody school standards and advocate other students to strive for excellence in everything that they do. Accordingly, students and school districts are forever changed by those who realize the value of athletic education.

Studies have shown, athletic participation is the greatest tool available to provide students with life-long skills of success. Positive character, health and wellness, and social and emotional intelligence are just a few of the benefits which allow students to win on and off the court. Despite the tremendous takeaways athletics supplies, most are using this powerful tool incorrectly—or not using it at all.

A Proponent and A Product

As I mentioned earlier, I'm not just a proponent of using sport to change lives but I'm actually a product of it. Athletics completely transformed my character as a youth and has provided the resources, experiences, and tools I use daily to be at my best.

At the age of 12, my Parents made a decision that forever changed the course of my life and the way I viewed athletics. I was a seventh-grader and in love with the game of basketball. But my school coaches failed to grasp how much sports mattered to me. These Coaches treated the game as though it were a game of Monopoly, randomly deciding playing time based on arbitrary factors. This confused me, because although I was committed to becoming the best I could be, my hard work seemed to not pay off and I never received feedback why. Rather than becoming dedicated to sport, I became dejected by it. For all the good sports had generated in my life; this one situation caused me to want to quit sports altogether. It's true that there is a thin line between love and hate!

Nevertheless, this school I attended was a top-tier academic school in the area. Parents would move heaven and earth to relocate into this district and provide their children with a premier education. Athletics was seen as unimportant in comparison with academics. Most parents gave little thought to the quality of the athletic education as long as the academic education was going well.

Contrary to this mindset, my parents made the decision to prioritize the athletic component of my education and moved me to another school. Although neighbors and friends were dumbfounded by the decision to leave; my Parents realized that athletics was not just important to me; athletics engaged me.

Experiencing an engaged education changed my life! Following the move, I was surrounded by educators who recognized the power of athletics and leveraged that power to promote my development. Being in an environment where my passion was matched by the adults around me, rocketed my commitment to an all-time high. This commitment not only applied to my athletic endeavors, but it poured into the classroom, my character, and in all other aspects of my life.

I went on to become my school's all-time leading scorer and have my jersey retired and hanging in the rafters. I also graduated third in my class, with a 4.6 GPA. But most of all, I came away with an example of how an engaged education can produce in students.

Students everywhere can also become engaged through sports. To be honest, math, science, and reading never engaged me. I did not lay awake in bed at night dreaming of becoming a successful mathematician or scientist. I did not wake up on Saturday mornings, to finish reading my favorite book. I was in love with sports and would do just about anything to be successful at it.

If academic subjects were your childhood motivation, you are a truly gifted person; but the simple fact is, most kids are not naturally motivated by non-physical endeavors. Beyond a natural attraction to athletics, Students are surrounded by external motivations as well. Any time they watch television, listen to advertisements, or read social media, sports are often the topic of the day. I want to see more schools leveraging this power to help students develop the skills and qualities needed to be successful at any endeavor.

This book is designed to help parents and educators *attract* student's attention and *align* them with successful habits. This can be accomplished through youth and school athletic programs. Whether dealing with students who love sport or those who could care less about it. Whether a student is age five or 15. Whether a student has had no previous experience, some experience, or loads of experience; this book will provide instruction, motivation, and clarity around designing transformational athletic experiences that produce positive life-enhancing results.

CHAPTER 3

WHAT IS ENGAGED ATHLETICS?

I f I could describe what Engaged Athletics is in one word, it would be *intentional*. Engaged Athletes and the adults who support them are intentional about using sports as a PRIMARY tool to motivate kids to be their best on and off the court. Perhaps it's easier to explain what is Engaged Athletics is *not*.

Engaged athletic programs are *not* the afterthought of successful school districts.

Educators of engaged athletic programs do *not* put sports on the back burner and allow their sports programs to settle for average.

Coaches of engaged athletics programs do *not* treat youth development as the least important element of the program.

Engaged athletes do *not* randomly miss practices and training due to fatigue or social events.

Hopefully you are beginning to see, Engaged Athletics is all about helping Students, Coaches, and Schools utilize athletics correctly to prepare kids for lifelong success. The issue arises when Schools, Coaches, and Parents fail to take advantage of this powerful tool. These groups are often lacking in what I call the 3 C's: Coaches do not balance competitiveness with teaching on Character. Parents (and students) do not possess the Commitment required to truly unlock the benefits of athletics. Lastly, Schools do not effectively help students seek out College scholarships.

It is my goal that this book will lead to effective use of athletics across all sports, activities, and age groups. Engaged Athletics is a call to action for schools and stakeholders to do their part to use this powerful tool while it is available and attractive to youth. The reality is, many kids will not even make their high school teams. Consequently, time is short to engage students using athletics. By acting now, we can equip every student with the skills needed for future success both on and off the court!

I will never forget the story of how my parents intentionally used athletics as a primary component of my development plan. I explained earlier how an engaged atmosphere changed my life. However, even as the stage got bigger my parents never lost sight of the fact that athletics was my key motivation.

As a Junior in high school, I had become one of the highest recruited basketball players in the State. A "who's who" of college coaches began to write and call. Bill Self, now famous University of Kansas Coach, was then at the University of Tulsa (TU) and had recruited me since my freshman year.

One evening as part of the recruiting process, Coach Self visited my home and joined my family for dinner. Following a lovely meal prepared by my mother (my dad will tell you, Mom hasn't cooked like that since I was in school!), we ventured into my parents sitting room (this was the first time I had ever been able to enter the room, let alone sit on the pristine white couch!).

15

Coach Self then began to tell us how great a school TU was academically. He waxed philosophically about the extensive education I could receive if I chose TU.

Dad immediately stopped the presentation as it was just beginning. He told Coach Self that academics was a requirement; I had no choice but to earn good grades. But basketball, on the other hand, was something I *chose* to do. Because athletics was a choice, I participated only because I cared. The academic presentation was not necessary. Dad advised Coach Self to focus on what TU could provide athletically because academics was taken care of.

What cojones! Not only did my dad know the power of athletic education, he lived by it! This conversation taught me the power of prioritizing athletic engagement. Administrators, parents and even coaches are fearful of placing athletics right next to academics on the scale of importance. Our society looks at parents who do so like gold diggers seeking the illicit riches of professional athletics, but this should not be the case. My parents prioritized athletics, because it was what engaged me. But they used athletics to get me to do my best in everything outside of athletics. You see athletics can lead to outstanding academics, phenomenal character, and unmistakable passion; yet, it starts with placing a priority on the areas where students are engaged.

Millions of kid's genuinely care about athletics. Parents and educators know the difficulty of earning the attention of young adults. Let's use athletics to get them to care about everything else! The trick is intentionality. If we can lay the bait that hooks them to truly care about athletics, we can attach and ascribe care to areas that stretch well beyond the field and court.

TO BE IN THE GAME. HAVE AN END GAME

Recently, a Parent told me that it was his goal for his son to receive a college scholarship. He did not care what sport, level, or school, but without a doubt wanted his son to receive free or reduced educational expenses for college.

Now you probably instantly feel some type of negativity about this dad and his outlandish goal for his son, but I actually think it is a great thing. You see most Parents and Students are just going through the motions of athletics. Signing up for teams and showing up for practices and games, without specific intentions regarding what they want to get out of it.

It is a shame that Parents/Students who set meaningful goals are looked at as crazies for intentionally pursuing athletic achievement.

Compare this to academics. How would you feel if he said, 'I want my son to receive a college academic scholarship of some sort'? Ah, that's better right? That is a culturally acceptable goal we can all cheer for!

But why!? If his student is truly engaged through athletics (and he is, by the way); why would we not set meaningful goals to make the most of student engagement? Most athletic participants are naive or afraid when it comes to setting goals for athletics. Yet, having an end game is the very first step to becoming an Engaged Athlete.

You see goals set the tone and determine the course of everything your student will do as an athlete. Her level of commitment, choice of programs, resilience, determination, skill-development, etc. will all be a function of the end goal. It's hard to imagine that many Parents/Students are operating without a rudder going wherever the athletic tide takes them. Lack of goals is a huge reason for the lack of commitment prevalent in youth athletics. Parents and Students are afraid to go all in because they are afraid of being held accountable to a particular goal.

Here are some tips to help you set goals and start your journey to become an Engaged Athlete. To set proper goals, think SMART: Specific, Measurable,

Achievable, Relevant, Time-Bound (Management Review by George T. Doran, 1981).

Specific - Whether your goal is based on performance, health and wellness, social and emotional skills or character, boil it down to what is most meaningful for you and your student. Becoming a Varsity starter, performing well under pressure, controlling his/her emotions, improving academics are a few examples of takeaways that may be important to some.

Measurable - Measurement often relates to numbers, and this is the difficult part about athletics. Other than statistics, which are relegated by limited playing time; numeric forms of athletic evaluation are not readily available. Instead, think of measurement as how much more prevalent your goal becomes. For instance, if you are wanting to perform well under pressure, began to take note of how often the desired result occurs when the opportunity arises. This is how your goal can become measurable and provide accountability towards reaching it.

Achievable – make sure your goals are realistic.

Relevant - Do not make goals that do not matter to you. Your goals should inspire and invigorate you to action. Failing to accomplish them should hurt!

Time-Bound - Just as the game clock causes a sense of urgency, setting a time period does the same for your goals. Again, goals hold us accountable. Keying our goals to a particular time limit forces constant evaluation.

Students should have a yearly athletic goal, if not quarterly. Lofty goals are great, however, short-term goals, or goal-plans, often incite the most action. If your goal is to earn a college baseball scholarship, your goal plan may involve hitting 100 balls per day for three months. Now you have a specific goal that is measurable, achievable, relevant, and time-bound. Now you are becoming Engaged!

So how do students make the transition to becoming Engaged Athletes? (In as little as three easy steps, you will learn how to engage Students through athletics and forever change lives.

Step 1 - Train

If you are not training, you are just playing. Engaged Athletics is all about going from simple participation to intentional involvement. All production has a process. Your mom's famous casserole, whipping your body in shape, and mastering your profession, all require time and focus toward a definite end. Training is the process that produces all takeaways you want to receive through athletics. Commitment is the skill that unlocks all other skills and is developed through training.

If you are an engaged athlete; you train—period.

First, let me explain why training is important. Training exponentially increases student development and success. As a result, he/she will become more committed or 'hooked' to athletics. Once hooked, discernable traits begin to develop. Trained students will begin to increase in their commitment, focus, and grit to overcome setbacks. This develops a sense of purpose and identity which causes and also enhances social and emotional intelligence. As a result, students' relationships, experiences, and connections will be enhanced.

ONLY PROCESS PRODUCES RESULTS

We live in the age of instant access. Companies are making millions by providing things faster and with less hassle. We can get food, entertainment, or even a home loan in an instant. As a result, our society has developed an intense disrespect for the process required for excellence.

Unfortunately, most parents believe just signing their

kids up for a team sport is enough. Some will go beyond that and will find a trainer for their child. Yet, the Parents remain unengaged in the process or the child lacks the motivation. These microwave strategies produce the opposite effect of Engaged Athletics. Rather than developing discipline, youth develop a lukewarm, uncommitted attitude, falsely believing they can master any endeavor without effort, concentration, or commitment.

Process can be costly and at times no fun. It can require participants to make tough decisions about how, when and where to spend their time, effort and resources. But process produces power.

Students who focus on process have little time for distractions. These students also demonstrate an ability to commit and adapt to goals despite opposition. Nearly every successful person has achieved success through process. Be willing to allow the pressures athletics involves (i.e. time-management, competition, and expectations) produce high-performing students.

These are just a few of the takeaways when using sports as a driver of student success. What's transformational is that these skills extend beyond athletics. <u>Engaged Athletes produce character and abilities that students otherwise would not exercise in their youth.</u> As a result, En-

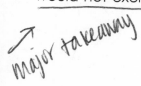
major takeaway

gaged Athletes are more developed, in a multi-tude of areas, than their peers. ⌐

Next, let's define training. Training is dedicated practice time set apart from team practices. Many incorrectly assume training and team practice are the same. This is why training sets Engaged Athletes apart. High achieving students and professionals take their work beyond the normal hours of the work day. High performers dedicate some personal time, outside of school or work, to internalize material that cannot be fully absorbed during the hustle and bustle of group activity. Investing your own time involves a higher-level of commitment most aren't willing to give.

Although training involves going above the normal work level, it does not necessarily require hours upon hours of intense work. Certainly at some point far along in the process, training may take on this aspect, but initially, training can be as little as 30 minutes a week. People trying to get in shape don't begin with intense workouts day after day. Instead, they begin with baby steps. A few sets of pushups; a brief walk.

Similarly, your child's training should start off short, easy and fun!

Now that we know what training is, the next logical question is *how* do you train? First, training must be consistent. Creating a weekly training schedule creates consistency, which in turn creates momentum.

My daily scheduled writing time provides me with a consistent rhythm toward my goal of writing this book. Even my body and circumstances have adapted to this daily ritual. I have not always been an early riser, but as a result of my consistency to this endeavor, early mornings are no longer as difficult as they once were.

Consistency also creates accountability. If you do fall off the training wagon, you will be able to retrace your steps. But in the event your consistency is intact, you have a strong sense of what you have accomplished.

Training should also be preplanned with each workout having a particular goal or theme. Just as we develop large goals for lengthy time periods, each training session should have a goal for the day. Focus towards improving a technical aspect, conditioning or general athleticism. The truth remains, without a goal, we are subject to getting lost. Get the most from your training by developing weekly or daily goals for each session.

Step 2 - Find your Tribe

Once training is adopted, Engaged Athletes must next find a tribe. Tribes are groups of people on our same path. These are usually found in the form of teams or workout groups. While training prepares; tribes test the quality of preparation. Training serves as internal accountability; tribes provide external accountability.

Coupling training with a tribe is where most miss the mark. Very few students do both. Students usually practice a lot on their own and become so comfortable that they fail to reach out to others. Alternatively, some students put all their hope in a tribe and never set aside time to train.

Tribes can provide transformational relationships that stimulate growth. Just knowing that others are pushing towards a particular goal provides motivation to accomplish our own. Overcoming similar struggles can even create deeper connections. Whether it's a Coach, Trainer or teammate, tribes engender relationships that inspire and engagement.

Step 3 - Tweak

Evaluation is a natural component to all that we do. We commonly assess learning, performance, and even finances. However, few take the time to assess athletic engagement. This is why students, teams, and programs fall behind over time. When was the last time you truly took inventory of a particular student's growth as a person and a player?

It's necessary that you assess the situation at each level of development. Every 4-6 months student growth should be evaluated. When growth is not present, students may be in need of new training techniques or a new tribe.

What Training Looks Like:

Training is not restricted by age and should begin as early as the age of three! We teach reading and counting at three, right? The young mind is ripe for learning and can easily soak up concepts at this age.

When my son, Jace, was three, we would 'train' outside or in the living room each week for 30 minutes. To him, it was playing with Dad. Little did he know; each game had a purpose. We would race, chase each other and kick, catch and fetch balls. We would even finish each day with him sprinting through cones and into my arms where I would toss him like a rocket into the sky! He loved it, just like he loved playing ABC and 123 games. As Parents, we had an intentional plan for his continued athletic growth.

A year later, I placed my son on a YMCA team where he began to develop context and confidence. He began to realize that his ability to get to the ball and pick it up faster than others led to more time with the ball in his hands, which he loved (who wouldn't!). His ability to run around cones also helped him run around defenders and get to the basket or goal. Most importantly, he realized that there were scores of other kids his age who loved to run and chase balls just like him. He not only made friends, but also got hooked on sports. Lastly, we take a hard look at his growth every few months. Sometimes he's ready to move forward, and honestly, sometimes he needs a step back. Either way, we do what is best for him at the time.

As a result of this simple system, Jace became an Engaged Athlete and continues to remain engaged through athletic participation. What I am most proud about is that at the age of 10, he is goal-oriented and intentional about his process to accomplish goals. He still enjoys being a kid and attending sleepovers, birthday parties, and playing video games. What started with 30 minutes per week has grown to 2-3 hours, however, this time of intentional focus has ingrained positive character traits that will benefit him for years to come.

The engaged system should also apply to your child's academics. Set aside a specific time, outside of school time and homework time, to hone academic skills and you will engage them in the classroom as well!

For those without a plan or group in place, start with individual training for 30 minutes once per week, and place your child in a local recreational (Church, YMCA) league. Stay consistent and you will see engagement in as little as 3-6 months. If nothing else, this creates great bonding between parents and children. Of course, there is much more work to be done. But this teaser can give your child a boost toward maximizing their potential to even higher levels.

CHAPTER 4

WHY YOU ARE NOT USING ATHLETICS CORRECTLY

Now that we know the steps to truly engage students through athletic participation, let's address some common mistakes which prevent athletics from being the effective growth tool that it can be. Most parents and coaches, including myself, are lacking in one of two distinct areas. Those of us who recognize the power of athletics are often limited by our experiences. We have become so restricted by how sports have been presented to us that we have lost sight on how sports should properly be used.

How are most adults not utilizing athletics correctly? Most of us are lacking in the two C's:

Character or Commitment. These are two foundational takeaways that are required to leverage athletic education. Using athletics without focusing on these key traits is like eating the meat and potatoes but skipping the vegetables and water. These fundamental nutrients actually help you absorb the meal! To help Student's absorb the benefits of athletic participation, Character and Commitment should be at the forefront of an athletic curriculum.

Character

How often do you as a parent, coach or educator focus on character as it results to athletics? Do you consistently and actively speak on the character takeaways involved in the athletic experience? How often do you place priority on character even if it comes at the expense of winning?

COACHES VS. PARENTS

Think back to a time in your life when you were at your best. Whether it was becoming intentional about something you wanted or wanted to become (i.e. character improvement, professional success, health gains, etc.); or a time when you were simply performing at an extremely high level; it is very likely that during this time you had a coach of some sort.

Maybe it was your parent, a mentor, a business coach, or even a motivational guru that you followed.

It is every parent's responsibility to lay a foundation of success for their child. Consequently, every parent must see themselves as a life coach of sorts. Yet, every coach also stands in the stead of a parent - In loco parentis - when students are in their care (us lawyers love to throw around legal jargon!).

As such, every parent is a coach and every coach is a parent to the students they supervise. However, these two groups rarely treat each other with mutual respect. Many coaches who have the benefit of years of experience dealing with students and parents of all types, let their ego rule the day instead of using this knowledge to help navigate parent relationships.

On the other hand, parents, who know the difficulty of dealing with with one child, can very easily imagine what it would be like to to have to manage dozens. Yet, parents condescend coaches and fail to communicate vital information about their student to the coach. This negatively affects the coach and the entire team. Parents need to exercise more regard for the group while coaches should exercise more regard for each individual. Parents and coaches need to be more intentional about working together to create Engaged Athletes.

Inserting character education can seem difficult and hokey even to me. But it is also difficult to teach a spread offense, base-running scheme or whatever system your team employs. We all can agree that character takeaways are the only lasting tools that stick with students throughout their lives. Anything this important should be prioritized.

I was an Engaged Athlete from the age of 12 to the age of 28 when my professional career ended. That amounts to 16 years dedicated to a particular sport. While the accolades and achievements were nice, none of them could pay bills. However, the character I developed continues to drive my success each and every day. Long hours in the gym gave me a stringent work ethic. Playing for many different teams across four separate countries, gave me an ability to interact and work well with various groups of people. Performing in NCAA Tournaments games attended by 20,000+ people equipped me with a penchant to execute under pressure.

All of these takeaways existed, yet I was unaware. I spent over a year in depression and loss of identity once my career ended. Had someone taught me about the character I had developed, I would have more likely recognized my strengths off the court and maintained my confidence, regardless of what was next. The fact is, most Engaged Athletes do not realize how athletics has positively shaped their lives beyond stats, awards, and wins.

It is no coincidence great coaches like Vince Lombardi, John Wooden, Pat Riley, and Phil Jackson are known primarily for their character education and secondly for winning. Teaching character helps students come to know their true selves. Character education helps build positive habits and ostracize negative ones. Students presented with character education are forced to take a hard look in the mirror and become accountable to certain standards. This leads to greater personal and external awareness.

How can you leverage this significant opportunity? The great news is tons of programs exist which help coaches implement pre-packaged character training. Many great examples are listed in the Resources section of the book. Parents and Coaches can utilize these tools to learn how to impart character education in the home or with their teams.

However you choose to implement it, become intentional about setting aside time to teach character. I know a high school Football Coach who has multiple State Championships. Everyday before practice, his team takes ten minutes in the film room to watch a particular character video. Not only is his team extremely successful on the field, but off the field as well. In an era where performance-enhancing drugs, sexual harassment, bullying, hazing, and alcohol abuse are prevalent at the high school level; students need something to counteract the variety of pressures they face.

Character messaging will definitely not engage all students, however, it will fundamentally change the lives of many, making it a significant subject we can not afford to disregard. Where else will students pickup character education? Church? Most will not attend or pay attention. School? Not a part of the regular curriculum. Social groups? Peers do not promote the message (have you seen what kids post on Instagram!?).

As coaches and educators we must begin to recognize character education as a primary responsibility. This is our key to promoting long-lasting positive effects in each student's life, despite what level of athlete they will ever become. New programs and methods of application make this easier to plug into our daily regimens to create lasting change.

Commitment

While coaches primarily lack in the *character* component; students and parents primarily lack in the *commitment* component. Commitment is showing up day after day no matter what gets in the way. The power of commitment cannot be magnified enough. Ample examples of the payoffs of commitment abound in our daily lives.

Have you ever seen a person in great shape and asked them their secret? They usually say they are not doing anything special, just simple things like, cutting out soda, walking a mile a day or lifting weights regularly. But probe further and you will find that they complete these simple actions with a relentless consistency. Their habits have become a lifestyle rather than a fad diet or fast track workout plan.

Similarly, the missing element to athletic success for most kids and parents today is a relentless commitment to development. Students will miss training, practices, and games for any reason from friend's birthday parties to grandma's graduation! When practices get hard or the season comes to a grind and things are not perfect, players (and sometimes parents!) check out mentally/and or physically.

Have you ever committed to a goal (i.e., not eating sugar, not cursing, working out five days/wk) and experienced results? What happened the one day you didn't follow through on your commitment? It disrupted the process, right? Hopefully, you felt bad and made up for it the next day. But often the disruption disconnects the process and leads to discontent. Discontent causes the sense of purpose and urgency to lessen. Questions like: 'Am I really losing weight?' or 'Is this even worth it?' began to creep in and before you know it focus on the goal is lost or decreased.

After my professional basketball career ended, I developed a successful basketball training business and served over 50 clients ranging from age eight to 18. It became commonplace to see parents and students fail to attend regularly after 5-6 weeks. Most of these students had a great chance to impact their lives using athletics, had they just stuck to the goal. As a former athlete whose special talent was hard-work, I can attest to the value they are leaving behind.

View commitment as the drop of water in the bucket that eventually leads to an overflow (results). Constantly disrupting the process causes the water to evaporate before it can reach the top! True commitment (showing up day after day) can be the hardest part of the process. However, it also produces the most life-changing results!

MASTER THE MUNDANE

New endeavors often begin with initial exuberance. New relationships, jobs, cars, and clothes. But what happens when initial exuberance wears off? Commitment is important because it helps students develop a staying power throughout the challenging and not so fun days. Every undertaking becomes mundane at some point. The key is to tap into your passion to push through.

The ability to master the mundane allows marriages to thrive, careers to grow, and commitments to last. Relentless consistency teaches students that even when the 'fun' wears off for a while, we must find joy in the process. 'The process is the way!'

If commitment is not your cup of tea, you not only are missing out on the benefits it provides; instead, you are actually reinforcing the habits of unsuccess. Yes I said it, unsuccess! Lack of commitment produces flakiness and an inability to make decisions. I've seen it time and time again. Pamela has a lot of homework and doesn't show (or even call) to practice. Inevitably, this habit creeps into other areas and Pamela never commits to excellence because any excuse will do. While this is an extreme example, realize that we are what we practice and small habits lead to big results. When students develop the tendency of checking out at the first sign of discontent, they use it as a coping mechanism whenever things get hard.

Establishing commitment forms a habit of success. <u>Committed athletes become committed people</u>. Not only will they commit to athletics, but they become more committed in other pursuits as well. Down the line, their enhanced ability to commit will prove positive in areas of their profession, marriage, faith, and beyond.

No coach expects 100% attendance. Things will come up and breaks (family vacations, downtime, other endeavors, etc.) should even be scheduled from time to time. However, these should not become frequent occurrences. Laying these dates out in advance provides coaches with much-appreciated notice and helps students develop commitment.

Here are a few tips to help parents and students solidify commitment:

Just say 'No'

Often we allow outside distractions to dictate our schedule. However, declining to take part in events which conflict with practices and games establishes the importance of athletics to your student in a meaningful way. I know work colleagues who will not take calls or emails on certain days like vacations or Sundays. This intentionality about how they will use this specific time establishes its importance and leads to an enhanced experience.

Begin to think of your child's training and practice times as off limits. Exercise commitment toward their development.

Synergize the grind

When commitment to youth athletics becomes a lifestyle, its important to capitalize logistically based on time, location and opportunities surrounding athletic participation. Packing a lunch or preparing dinner the night before makes the process more efficient. Workouts and practices can often run later into the evening, so completing homework, chores, etc. before can be a big help.

This also teaches students how to balance responsibilities while still pursuing their goals. Many people let life get in the way of their purpose. Equipping your child to pursue purpose despite distractions is a tremendous skill that will dictate future success. All of our kid's practices and workouts are in the evening. My wife and I synergize our grind by preparing lunch and dinner the night before and packing clothes so they are ready to go. I also schedule times throughout the week to batch projects from work, business and life. As a result, we are not often overwhelmed by our commitment to athletics.

Because amateur athletics often take place on weekends, conflicts with religious practices can occur. We also schedule our weekly spiritual time. Attending an earlier church service or setting aside time to read, pray and reflect as a family is important to us. Synergizing and scheduling other important components also furthers commitments in those other areas and places a high value on them for our children.

Push past conflicts

Temptation is always at the door ready to receive you with open arms. Whether the temptation to sleep in, eat the donut, or binge watch a favorite show; plenty of temptations exist, aimed at disrupting your consistency. Beyond that, life does happen. Colds/flu, dentist visits, car trouble, etc., can all cause disruptions to the process. However, it is extremely powerful when you persevere despite these temptations and random conflicts.

Developing youth is a long journey, but the takeaways commitment provides students will produce a positive impact at some point in their lives. To think, this transformation will all be because you did everything in your power to be present each time there was an opportunity to improve.

Balancing the Two C's

I realize this outlook may seem extreme but as a parent and coach, I see coaches rarely teaching character and parents who are anything but committed. If you were writing a letter about life that your children would read 10 years from now, what are a few keys to success you would list? Most likely character and commitment would be at the top of the list.

Character unlocks order in life, and commitment is the only skill that unlocks all other skills. Character is an expression of internal consistency while commitment is an expression of external consistency. These two traits are essential to accomplishing any goal.

Other components of athletic participation and life are without a doubt important. However, if educators can increase character education and commitment by even 1%, more students will be engaged in athletics and forever changed.

Character is an expression of internal consistency

Commitment is an expression of external consistency

CHAPTER 5

SCHOOLS OF ENGAGEMENT

As an Educational Administrator, I often come across schools with a distorted view toward athletics. Some schools allow athletics to dictate too much of school culture, policy, and rules. This leads to trouble, creating coaches and teams that feel entitled, make up their own rules and administer their own version of justice.

Other schools virtually ignore their athletic programs. These schools allow issues to fester, non-professionalism to languish, and fail to acknowledge athletics as an important source of education and influence in their student's lives.

These divergent products leave stakeholders frustrated and unwilling to support athletics programming. In the midst of Federal and State budget cuts to education across the nation, many school leaders are considering throwing athletics into the fray.

However, we must not lose sight of the fact that athletics is an attention-grabbing force for students and families. The physical exertion, camaraderie, and community attention associated with sports programs causes students to want to engage and parents to seek out the best programs. When used correctly, athletics is an impactful educational magnet.

Educators must see school as a service. Ultimately, it is our role to serve clients. To do so, we must first attract those clients. Education without athletics is a service that disregards the needs of many students. Consequently, education becomes severely less in-demand when balanced education-based athletic programs are not a part of the puzzle.

Our on-demand world provides customers access to engaging content at all times. Not only is information prevalent, but choices are as well. Educational options include home-schools, transfers, online schools, boarding schools and athletic academies just to name a few.

To compete in this world and add value to customers, we must offer what intrigues them. Most educators believe technology is the most engaging tool we have at our disposal. They are not incorrect in this assessment; however, athletics and activities can be just as engaging if not more so! Physical movement and in-person interactions still maintain an organic appeal that trumps electronic engagement. When we hone the power of athletics, we can use it for the greatest good, to entertain and educate students to become their best selves.

How can you leverage the power of athletics to forever change your school culture?

Start with Coaches

Coaches are on the front lines of this process. Hiring quality coaches starts with an exhaustive search supported by stringent standards. Moral character and a passion for teaching students must flank this list. Next, the ability to connect with students and teach positive character ranks even above sport-specific coaching knowledge.

Find the right Coaches, impart the correct mindset and witness your school's culture begin to adapt. Partner coaches with resources and the freedom they need to educate beyond the court. Using coaches as the ignition switch allows schools to establish their culture and remain true to the values they uphold as a district.

Invest in Student-Athletes

Engagement exists where care resides. When students are surrounded by invested stakeholders, they too will invest at a higher level. This means not only must coaches be above par, but also logistics such as programming, facilities, and equipment. Let's move beyond decrepit buildings, dilapidated locker rooms, and decade-old uniforms. When schools demonstrate care in this regard, the impact can be incredible. When students have proper coaching and resources, it communicates that Districts care.

Building healthy athletic programs also promotes school culture and branding. This is because student-athletes are the most high-profile people within any school or community. When these students have been involved with positive character building programs they morph into a school's greatest advertisements.

Marketing is a key element to a successful business. The attention athletics garners both inside and outside the school amounts to substantial organic marketing. Schools that get intentional with this tool and craft messaging delivered by student-athletes are even more effective. Just take one look at how athletics drives student engagement on college campuses. This power is available at the secondary school level as well.

Connect with Community

Community is the final piece of the puzzle for using athletics as a driver to change school culture. Community includes District personnel and those outside the school. Community buy-in not only boosts the trajectory of school initiatives, but it expands the success bubble for students. When the community is on board with the school's direction for change, community members will begin to hold their sons, daughters, grandkids, neighbors, and friends to the standards that have been put forth by the school.

I urge Administrators wishing to implement worthwhile initiatives to take a hard look at how their athletics programs can be used to proliferate the proper message. Announcements at home games, Student-Athlete PSAs, and marketing tools can prove powerful.

The Role of Engaged Parents

Parents of Engaged Athletes must do their best to become aware of the schools which understand and leverage the value of athletic education. Unprofessional coaches, underserved athletes, and unkempt facilities/equipment are telltale signs. Know which schools and programs invest in offseason training to keep students engaged throughout the year. Look into the coach's method of interacting with past students. Is she concerned with helping students reach their goals, or just winning games and collecting a check?

Also be aware of schools that support athletics but fail to provide the necessary accountability measures. Many parents new to an area seek out the school with the most recent history of success in their sport of interest. Soon thereafter, they experience on-the-field success only to be derailed by a culture of negative character. Scandals often rock these programs because their students develop destructive habits. Scholarships are lost, coaches are let go and the process starts all over again.

The greatest voice you as a parent have, as it relates to education, is where you choose to send your student. As more parents select high performing education-based athletics programs, other schools will be forced to join the movement or be left behind. Do not be afraid to prioritize your child's athletic education. We can no longer devalue the role youth and school sports plays within student development. While it sounds taboo, parents would be remiss not to perform due diligence and become aware of the inputs that affect school athletic programs. Ultimately, these are important components that can propel or derail student's athletic engagement

CHAPTER 6

ENGAGED COACHES STAND UP

Nearly every coach began his or her coaching journey with the goal of helping students succeed. However, time, apathy, and disappointments can cause enthusiasm to fade. Coaches must fight to maintain student development as their primary mission because for many students athletics is (or can be) their 'why.'

Every human being is ultimately responsible for positively impacting others. Through our experiences, both positive and negative, we develop insight that allows us to teach best practices. This process moves and improves our world.

As coaches, you serve as leaders and guides to impressionable youth. Your guidance acts as a launching pad for young people to accomplish great things and shape our world in profound ways. I urge you to realize the impact you have on this Earth!

Your words and actions will inspire, inform and influence future generations; perhaps until the end of time. Make them meaningful!

First, realize that you as a coach are connecting with students in an area where they truly care about. We all know students can easily 'zone out' school, religion, and other forms of education spewed by adults. However, you hold the keys to the most popular form of entertainment in the world. You possess a phenomenal opportunity to use it to change lives.

Recognize the importance of your calling and use it to drive your passion. This means seeking excellence in your craft.

As an educator, I can say that education is a field where many professionals go to languish. Coaches, administrators, and school employees can go decades without seeking professional accomplishments or growth. This is often due to the constraints placed on educators by governing bodies, but I digress. With the world's most precious resource in our hands, many are sleeping on the job, stuck in mediocrity, or overwhelmed.

This also includes coaches. Teachers and administrators have accountability through Federal and State Education Department protocols, tests and certifications. These objective requirements, by and large, do not exist for coaches. Consequently, coaches are seemingly free to do what they want and grow according to their own desires or lack thereof. This has produced many coaches who are stuck in the past and refuse to grow. True, some things were better in the 'good old days' however, we have to find new ways to package those good things and present them afresh to today's youth.

How do you as a coach and key stakeholder in the process of developing youth, leverage athletics to forever change Student lives?

Here's how:

1. Protect Professionalism

One method of repackaging and re-presenting the message is to protect the professionalism of the coaching craft. Every profession has standards. However, the lack of accountability involved in youth and school sports leaves many to relax or disregard typical standards of professionalism. This cannot be. Remember, you are influencing the next generation in a major way. The way you talk, dress and interact with people will speak volumes and influence generations of student-athletes.

Beyond this, know that you and your school are a brand. Your actions, attitude, and achievements will speak volumes about what that brand represents. Even your dress doubles as brand packaging and communicates something to potential customers. Whether you seek personal growth, achievement, or maximizing your impact; your brand's reputation provides the leverage to unlock opportunity.

Every passing day and interaction is an exercise in building or destroying your brand. Below are a couple tips to help you create a strong personal brand that others want to buy in to.

Watch Your Words

Whether communicating instructions to players, giving a motivational speech, or casual conversation, know that your words are being measured. Too often, coaches are found cursing on sidelines, being explicit on social media, or sending taboo text messages.

Communication is the key to human interactions. Consequently, everyone is paying attention to how you communicate. Don't let the only one not paying attention to be you. Inattention to communication can be extremely costly in today's day and age. Name-calling, cursing, and explicit jokes can derail professional careers and blunt the impact coaches have.

Protect your professionalism by always keeping your words above-board, even when communicating amongst coaches. Never put an insult or offensive joke in writing. If you have an issue with someone, say it in person. Those things often get saved and reappear in the biggest moments of your career. Realize that how you speak on a daily basis can come to define you and your program.

Remember, we are what we practice. Practice watching your words on a daily and even hourly basis. Think back on different conversations throughout the day and how you could have approached them differently. Allow emotionally driven email and texts to sit for at least an hour before pressing send. Even take care in how you greet people when you enter a room.

Many coaches are introverted, bypassing students, parents, and others with less than a grumble. Coaches are leaders and many stakeholders depend on their guidance. Each interaction is an opportunity to influence, even if only with a smile or wave. Furthermore, parents and other stakeholders can become huge supporters of a coach's mission and even career. Take time to nurture your calling by communicating with care.

Dress for Success

We get it, you are a coach, you sweat, you yell, you run, but do you have to do it in rags? How you dress says a lot about you. Unwashed, old and ill-fitting clothing communicates something to others. To some, this demonstrates a lack of excellence or attention to detail. Many coaches quip 'I don't care about clothing, I care about kids.' However, recognize clothing is an important part of your packaging. People make most purchasing decisions based on the package. Do not allow your talents, purpose, and impact to be muted by unattractive packaging.

Change this perception by finding professional attire that suits your style. Whether business casual, clean-cut athletic wear, or more formal; dress as though your mission depends on it. Often it makes sense to have several outfits on hand to allow you to go from the boardroom to the sidelines seamlessly.

Reiterate this message by requiring your students to dress for success. Special attire for game days and events helps them realize that clothing communicates a mentality of professionalism and productivity. When we dress up we communicate we are on a mission toward a specific goal.

While it's easy to wake-up and throw on the first set of clean (or maybe not clean) sweats that we see. It is quite another thing to have a professional looking outfit (or a couple of them!) already picked out and ready to go for the day. Our dress is a representation of who we are or at least who we think we are. Dress for the job you want to have, the production you want to achieve, and the person you want to become.

Professional under Pressure

Although your mission is geared to athletics, your mission has influence beyond the court or playing field. Coaches have a platform that can influence people of all walks of life. Whether coaching on the sidelines or dealing with difficult situations, these interactions can often go viral and spread like wildfire. Ultimately, how coaches behave while under pressure leaves other with an impression about the coach, his team and even athletics as a whole. Know that your actions represent us all!

Coaches often find themselves in heated game situations or in difficult conversations with students, parents, or another educator. While these people are adults, coaches have a higher platform and direct influence over students who hang on their every word. How you act while under pressure will demonstrate your character and promote the values you hold dear. Others will come to see the value of athletic education based on your influence. Ultimately, your example will have lasting impact on the support of your program and athletics in general.

Prepare ahead of time for these pressures by using pressure releases like yoga, meditation, time outdoors, working out, family time, or whatever takes your mind away. I enjoy daily prayer and meditation to help me keep what's really important in front of my mind. This practice equips me to react correctly to difficult situations throughout the day. When I am tempted to yell, reply angrily, or become dismissive of others; I am able to react with a tactful response which correctly represents the values I hold dear.

Whatever helps you, make it a daily practice to get the full benefits it offers. With the hectic schedule and late nights involved in coaching it is necessary to employ stress-busting habits to be your best.

Never forget the platform and impact you have. Students and adults alike look up to you. Perfection is not the goal, but progression is. We are calling youth to be their best in every area, Coaches must adopt this approach as well.

2. Master your Craft

Our society looks up to those who master their craft. Michael Jordan's ability to take over a basketball game, Martin Luther King's ability to inspire a crowd, Einstein's ability to solve complex math issues, all came as a result of mastery.

Mastery is the process of developing knowledge or proficiency by putting in extra time. But oftentimes educators are so pressed for time and resources that we seek to become masters by doing rather than practicing. This is like preparing to ace the exam by just doing the classwork. 'A' students go beyond classwork and complete the homework, taking personal time to truly understand the content beyond memorization. Yet, so many educators rely solely upon what they have memorized over years. Disregarding that the content has evolved as have the methods to teach it.

Let's practice what we preach as educators and begin to truly master our craft. Mastery is a process that always begins with being intentional with our time. Michael Jordan did not accidentally end up putting up hundreds of shots per day, nor did Martin Luther King work on his speeches when he felt like it. People who are above average experts in their field, *schedule* in extra time. With such an important responsibility as producing better young people, it leaves little doubt that coaches should seek to master their craft and fulfill their mission as educators.

Grow with a Group

Groups have a way of taking us beyond our limits and providing external awareness. Through groups, we come to know the mindsets and missions of others, which can provide meaningful influence in our development. Groups also provide accountability and camaraderie. Aligning with others around common goals allows us to monitor our progress and establishes support throughout it.

Local Coaches' Associations, social media groups, or simply developing relationships with others in your sport, can supply the group support and network needed to improve. Working in isolation can drive you crazy. Lack of outlets can also cause you to become blindsided by emerging trends and information that could prove important to you or the students you lead.

Resume the Resume

Many coaches assume winning games is proof of their ability to coach. But winning is largely a function of player's skill levels as opposed to coaching skill. Even great coaches like Phil Jackson, Geno Auriemma and Mike Krzyzewski have all, coincidentally, enjoyed the luxury of coaching some of the greatest athletes of all-time.

As an Athletic Director, the ability to win games is an important factor whenever I set out to hire a coach. However, its only one piece of the puzzle. Educational background, coaching certifications, and professional development are also key components of the coach's reputation.

Coaches should have tangible proof of their prowess. Earning a college degree communicates that you are intelligent, trustworthy and consistent in execution toward a goal. Earning a Master's or a Doctorate demonstrates these same intangibles times ten! Coaching certifications indicate that a coach is committed to continual improvement. Additional professional development such as serving on a Board of Directors, national association, and attending conferences further establish credibility.

Many methods now exist which will allow you to acquire knowledge. From online schooling to remote certification programs all empower you to acquire knowledge in a way that works best with your situation.

Know that this information can cost money. However, do not let money be the reason you do not move forward in your craft. After a grueling two-year journey in law school, I was shocked to find out it would cost over $3,000 to take the bar exam! I thought they should be paying me! But I received good advice that barriers are laid down at the door of each profession to prevent those from entering who don't possess the willpower to overcome. Forking over $3,000 was not fun, however; the cost was nominal in comparison to the benefits having the certification has provided.

Do not be small-minded and think some person or group needs your money. Rather, acquire the tangible evidence that says you value learning and have lots to offer those you lead.

3. Connect Beyond

Despite all the bells, whistles and skills a coach may have; the most important skill any coach can have is the ability to connect with students. Even though sports are popular to most, even a child will turn down cake from a stranger.

Connecting with students beyond their interactions with you as an athlete sets the stage for transformation. Here are a few tips to go beyond the playing field to help unlock student potential.

Complement

Simply complimenting a student opens the door to conversation and getting to know more about them. Make it a practice to find something good to say about your students, especially those you tend to interact with less. As demanding coaches who constantly correct and critique, words of kindness go a long way.

Ask Questions

The world is constantly changing. The expected behaviors and actions of youth do not always follow what adults expect. Think about it, many youth today have less interpersonal interactions due to the internet. As a result, it takes them longer to figure out complex instructions, read body language, and asses situations. Asking questions will help provide you with insight into their thought processes and help you come to know what makes them tick.

Remember, you are a torch-bearer for athletic education. Your influence not only drives student-athletes but can affect Business people,

Pastors, Bankers, etc. to realize the value of athletic education and seek to get their children involved and offer support.

Never think your influence is relegated to the playing field. Your calling will affect people from all walks of life. Protect and nurture it to create the impact you are meant to have! Know that you as a coach, whatever the level, can become great at your craft and be recognized as one of the best to ever do it. However, people will not only remember your productivity, they will remember your character. As a teacher of character, practice on being the best person you can be, even when you think no one is watching.

CHAPTER 7

A TRAINING GUIDE FOR ALL AGES

L ack of commitment is the biggest problem eroding the landscape of youth athletics. Most students don't have a plan or process in place that helps them achieve their goal. Training is the linchpin to the process. However, realize that process often differs from end product; just as cake batter looks a lot different from a finished cake! Those who lack commitment derail the process and end up taking the cake out of the oven before it can fully cook. More parents and students must view training as the oven that can cause students full potential to rise.

Life-changing character traits such as hard work, grit, perseverance, self-awareness, and passion are readily available to all students involved in athletics and activities; but these traits are only unlocked when students truly deep-dive into the content. This deep dive is only accomplished by commitment to a process that takes students beyond rote participation.

Parents and students too often become luke-warm participants, going through the motions but never going beyond them. These partici-pants falsely believe they are developing life-skills and falsely expect on the field success. However, what is common amongst all success-ful athletes, no matter the level, is a relentless commitment to the process of training. These students are forever-changed because the life-skills were ingrained into them through a pro-cess, much like baking in an oven. Consequent-ly, these life-skills become deep-rooted and transformational; while those students without a process are left with shallow traits that never rise out of them, much like a no-bake pastry.

As I said before, if you are not training; you are just playing. Training is consistently setting aside dedicated practice time. Consequently, how much students should be training is an answer that is specific to each situation.

No magic formula exists but consistency is the common denominator to success. Two types of consistency are relevant: consistency in availability and consistency in motivation. Ask yourself two questions: 1) How often is my student available to train? 2) How much does my student want to train? Once these factors are identified, no matter the answer, find a training program that matches your response.

This is the great thing about training, any amount is transformational when combined with consistency. Small amounts, will lead to deeper understanding and application. Small amounts will also lead students to eventually seek larger amounts. It is like a positive drug!

Again, I urge you, to become an Engaged Athlete or an athlete that is developing the critical takeaways of athletic participation, get started with some type (any type!) of training program right away! Just getting started with this process will engender student's first steps towards mastery and forming unbreakable long-term habits.

Training is not about paying thousands of dollars or spending hours on end. Instead training is about unlocking tools that help students achieve success. Most people don't devote extra time to their craft. The ones that do quickly rise to the top. Establishing this habit in students in a bite-size and easy to swallow pill like sports, supplies them with an advantage in the game of life. Every minute of focused work toward the goal develops mastery and transformational character traits that will forever be ingrained inside that Student.

Below are some suggested training plans to help get you going.

Ages 3-10

Ages 3-10 should be balanced between local recreational leagues and parent training. Normal participation level involves one rec team practice per week, and one training of at least 30 minutes each week.

Kids aged 8-10 should be practicing with a rec or club team twice per week and working with a parent or coach on skill development for 30 minutes to one hour per week.

This regimen is recommended for at least nine months out of the year. The sports may change throughout the year, but students should be in-volved in a sport/activity and training for the majority of the year. Also, if your student does take a 2-3 month break from sports, have them continue to stay active. Swim, run, bike, etc. Three months of Playstation without movement will develop negative character traits and erase much of what has been developed.

Realize that exceptions exist to every rule. Some parents will end up transporting their six-year-olds across the country for games and tourna-ments! Outliers engaged above this prescribed level will always exist, rather right or wrong, (see chapter on burnout) however; remember each training regimen ultimately depends on the stu-dent's engagement and the amount of in-volvement which intrigues them.

On the other hand, many parents do not partic-ipate even at this minimal level. As a result, their students are ill-equipped to realize future athlet-ic success and the takeaways that come with participation in youth and high school sports.

This is the first step in a long process. There is no need to overdo it, but we must provide a proper foundation. Preparing youth for future success is a fundamental parental duty. This duty cannot be fully realized if athletics is not in the picture. Think of this first step as the athletic equivalent of ABCs and 123s.

No matter the level of participation selected, the decision should not be based solely on what parents want. Students involved in advanced levels of participation should first evidence a willingness to do more. Otherwise, stick with the process and maintain a regular participation level until desire increases.

While some will thrive at advanced levels of participation at this age level, burnout is a constant risk. As kids age, the commitments increase. Not only will over-trained student-athletes exhibit less improvement gains, the increased commitment at later stages could eventually overwhelm kids.

Recreational leagues are those that prioritize participation versus competition at all costs. The YMCA, Salvation Army, and local churches come to mind. These leagues are optimal at this level, however, you may live in an area which has unorganized recreational leagues. In this case, club level participation may make sense, however, know that making the jump to club can quickly and unexpectedly escalate to overdoing it. If you are moving forward with the club option in this age group, seek out club teams that are primarily playing locally and promote character and skill development over winning championships.

Lastly, training at this age can often be as simple as throwing and catching a ball, playing racing games, or even dodgeball! Athleticism builders such as soccer and gymnastics are excellent foundations for any future sport choice. As students reach the eight year-old mark, training should become more regimented, with scripted drills and such. However, the key at this age is to get them moving and developing general athletic skills.

Ages 10-14

Participation rate takes a jump at this stage. At this point, parents and students need to view athletic participation as an absolute necessity. On level is school or club team practices two or three times per week, plus one to two days of training for an hour each session. Club participation is recommended at this level; especially during the off-season for students on school teams. This level of participation and training should take place 10-11 months out of the year. This is because the majority of youth development occurs during this stage. Month-long breaks should not occur, however; you can find breaks throughout the year by taking a week off here or there.

Although this amount of activity will seem over-whelming to busy parents, this is a pivotal age for high school preparation. Keep in mind that high school teams practice at least 5-6 days per week, not to mention club participation. To pre-pare student for this high rate of activity, the foundation must be laid at this age level.

Club teams in this age group should be traveling and exposing students to advanced competi-tion. Training sessions should now include a pro-fessional trainer or someone with a high level of playing and/or coaching experience. Addition-ally, skills training should be switched with per-formance training on a quarterly basis. This means skill-building drills should be rotated with those which focus on foot-speed, strength train-ing and cardiovascular conditioning for a few weeks at a time.

If your student is on the outside looking in when it comes to finding a club team, rec is still an op-tion, but a consistent training schedule should be followed. You may also try practicing with a club team, or playing as an alternate from time to time when a club team is missing players due to vacations or other conflicts.

HOW LONG SHOULD YOU COACH YOUR KIDS

Many parents are often anxious when it comes to stepping in and coaching kids at a young age. They are afraid that they do not know enough or are un-comfortable leading impressionable youth. Youth athletics before Junior High (6th/7th grade) deals mostly with teaching consistency and character, something all high-functioning adults are capable of doing. Developing simple goals for the season and a few practice plans (Youtube some drills if need be!) will prepare any parent to become a stellar youth coach.

Parents should look to get involved in coaching youth sports for the camaraderie it provides with their student and their peers. This is a parent's chance to peek behind the curtain and find out how their student reacts in a variety of circumstances, like getting a chance to sit in on their class. Most importantly, coaching your student is a great way to identify her particular strengths and weaknesses; an important factor in later development.

Despite these great assets, coaching your student beyond elementary age can become detrimental. First, variety is the spice of life. Changing teachers helps accentuate various aspects of development.

Any student with the same teacher from 1st-9th grade will naturally be underdeveloped. This is even the case with good coaches. Despite being a former Division-I athlete, professional athlete and coach for every level from grade school to high school; I am doing my student a disservice if I am their only coach throughout their development.

Secondly, you do not know everything! It's not a positive thing to develop yourself as the only voice your student believes or trusts. This may be a valuable boost of self-esteem for parents, but this sets up students for future life issues. Students must remain pliable and maintain the ability to adapt to various styles of coaching. In essence, students must value and adapt to many teachers over the course of their athletics education; prepare them early by allowing them to hear different voices.

Lastly, you should not coach your student past elementary because middle school matters. Middle school is the priming ground for high school. Your student should come to adapt to real-world scenarios during this three to four year process. Whether it is a new coach, the level of competition, or a different style of play; middle school is an opportunity to take the training wheels off and truly gauge where your student stands.

Middle school or Junior High represents a great time period to introduce professional coaches and trainers. These people are knowledgeable regarding working with students in this age range and have established a curriculum to help them reach prescribed levels. Interacting with external mentors will also help motivate and renew your student's athletic passion. Retiring your whistle at or near this age also allows you to focus on your student rather than an entire group. This is when knowing your student's strengths and weaknesses (told you this would be important!) will allow you to make the best use of new teaching and principles.

Of course, there are exceptions to every rule, you may need to step in on a certain team that needs a coach, or perhaps you yourself work as a Junior High or High School coach of some sort. However, by and large, students are best served when parents discontinue coaching at the middle school level.

Age 14-18

Like it or not, parents must realize that the barriers of athletic entry increase in high school. Consequently, students should be primed for 7th and 8th grade participation to create momentum as they enter high school. Prioritize building confidence, character and sport-specific skills within this age range to prepare your student for high school success.

The suggested commitment for this level is participation on a school as well as club team paired with two to three days of training per week. School teams will practice daily and club teams actually practice less and play more during this period. Unfortunately, some coaches at this level prioritize winning over development, which causes students to fall behind in their personal growth. This is where consistent personal training enables many students to take a huge step in their preparation.

PLAYING TIME

This age group marks a difficult decision for coaches. They generally have a short window of time, limited minutes to give, and a large contingent of athletes. Some schools base who makes the team and gets minutes based on who is the oldest. I refer to these schools as 'wait your turn' programs. Wait your turn programs are great for slower developing kids, who need a couple years to watch, absorb and become comfortable at the Varsity level.

Other athletic programs employ what I call an 'athletes first' mentality. They play the best athletes regardless of age or how long they have even been with the program. These programs are great for young phenom athletes and transfer students, who perhaps were not playing at other schools.

Both types have pros and cons. Wait your turn programs may not provide ample opportunity for younger standout athletes. While athletes first programs may disregard older students needs and opportunities for new younger talent. Admittedly, some programs may be flexible enough to integrate a little of both styles.

As a parent, it is important to know the methods that your high school programs employ so you can prepare your child accordingly. Promising freshman may be thrust into a role they are not prepared or perhaps not even make the varsity team. Seniors may be saddled with leadership duties or alternatively receive less minutes as coaches prepare younger players for the following year. The program structure can have significant implications.

Know that these decisions are difficult for coaches. Playing time and roles are determined by a complex set of factors which constantly change. These decisions can only be made according to the Coach's unique digression, based on his or her evaluation on the team as a whole and not solely based on who are the best players. No matter the case, realizing this dynamic up front will help parents and students maintain a clearer perspective throughout their high school athletic journey.

We can all understand that commitment has profound impact even in our lives as adults. Whether it be our relationships, religious walk or even our careers, commitment helps us to reach new levels. Similarly, commitment to maximizing athletic education will produce phenomenal results in students. Although it can become overwhelming, none of us would blink when it comes to applying greater commitment to student's academic education. Yet both are vital to long-term success. Both are necessary to produce well-rounded individuals, and both are part of our duty to provide to youth today. Find the training regimen that is right for your student[s] and get ready for positive change to occur!

CHAPTER 8

AVOIDING BURNOUT

Now that you have an idea what real athletic engagement looks like, let's discuss how to avoid burnout and help students stay engaged over the long-haul. Many adults believe we should let 'kids be kids' and give them ample idle time to do whatever comes to mind. Realize that letting kids be kids also means engaging them through responsibilities which prepare them for adulthood. That's simply part of being a kid. So don't be anxious because Jennifer has constantly increasing responsibility and accountability through sport. It's life! And, she is learning responsibility and habits that will make her successful where she can have plenty of paid vacations as an adult!

Still, the key to athletic engagement is *engagement*. We want to keep youth engrossed in activity so the process does not feel like one. Here are some tips to keep it fresh.

Don't Overwhelm

Too much too soon can cause a burden that turns students away from sport. Parents, more so than students, are often in a rush to escalate. Remember the recommendations of the previous chapter; when students have a consistent foundation of training throughout their youth, the foundation can always be built upon as the motivation grows. Take your time and allow your student to fully develop on each stage before inorganically jumping to a higher level.

I made the mistake of doing too much too soon with my son, Jace.

Jace loved sport at an early age. In fact, he was so smitten by basketball and soccer that at the age of four, while his friends were watching cartoons, he was watching countless hours of throwback NBA reruns and MLS soccer games! Naturally, as an athlete myself, I had a plan to make the most of his intrigue.

Jace started in recreational leagues at the age of four. He had immediate success, because he knew more than most. It was not unusual for Jace to score all of his team's points or goals. Of course, it was my great decision to begin to 'push' Jace out of his comfort zone and to a higher level (at the age of four, mind you!)

The following season, I placed Jace in a higher age group, with kids one to two years older than him. He quickly became frustrated when he could not get to the ball or score points. This lead me to activate my elite skills of instruction to 'coach him up' and out of this funk he had found himself in. As Jace and I trained in preparation for game success, I assumed he would automatically apply these skills in the game. When he did not, due to being the most inexperienced kid on the court, I then resorted to yelling at him for each and every mistake.

It wasn't long before Jace was telling me he did not want to go to practices or games. I, the super-athlete dad and advocate of all things sport, had actually caused my son to not like them! What a bummer! It is one thing for a kid to not like sports, but it's altogether something different when you the parent are the cause of it.

We took a step back (I stopped yelling as much!) and joined a quasi-club level team which participated in mix of club tournaments and rec leagues and his vigor for the game returned. Although, at the age of 10, he has become very effective on the club scene, we still participate in rec leagues a couple months out of the year. It allows him to have fun and demonstrate how far his skill has advanced. It also gives him the opportunity to help others with less advanced skill sets, which develops his leadership skills.

However, if your student is participating at the recommended level, do not be fooled that because he is dominant at the rec level he is the next Michael Jordan or Lebron James. Parent's social media pages feature countless highlight reels of their 10-year-olds most amazing plays. However, participants at this level have such varying degrees of skill level, that many of the opponents they face are little more that blinking mannequins. As a result, parents should not be overly excited about how good their child is at a young age.

Parents can get caught up in this success and fail to further prepare students, because they see them as 'ahead.' Success is a positive thing when it motivates students toward greater commitment in the pursuit of more success. Parents, keep taking videos, but instead use them to break down the positive and negative aspects of the play, with a focus towards improvement.

Prioritize Process

'Trust the Process' has become a popular cry of many sports fans all over the world. Students, schools, and stakeholders would do well to adopt this same approach. Many fail to adopt a process because they don't have goals established which chart their course. Goals will keep you on the path of a process rather than disrupting growth at every impediment or wave of influence.

Parents should establish goals for students on a yearly if not bi-yearly basis. Goals like 'become best hitter in the conference;' 'controlling emotions in the clutch;' or 'winning a state championship' will be flanked by goal plans which will help manifest intended results.

Once goals and plans are established, one way to know if you have a process is if you are training consistently. As I said in Chapter 4, training is the process necessary to help you reach any goal in life, including athletic ones. Training will bring about positive results, which entail positive emotions, which bring about engagement.

However, burnout occurs when process is short-circuited and too much faith is placed in a team. Upon finding a team many mistakenly believe all of their student's deficiencies will be automatically solved. Too many parents view this as an a opportunity to disengage and just 'let the coach handle it.' When a student begins to decline and disengage because of particular needs and weaknesses not being addressed, that parent is the last to know and first to be upset.

A team alone cannot prepare any student for their next level of development; just as a class alone cannot fully prepare a student for their next level. More resources must come into play to leverage the power of engaged teaching. Teams come and go throughout their career; training, however, is a constant companion. The majority of any coach or teacher's time is invested in the team/class as a whole rather than individual improvement. Coaches focus on teaching the team to manage situations collectively. Little time is left over to tackle the nuanced deficiencies of each student. This makes individual improvement a weekly responsibility of the Engaged Athlete.

Remain engaged as a parent and continue to supplement what students lack through training. Communicate with coaches for updates on your student's progress just as you would with their teacher. Training will allow your child to continue to grow, even if you have lapses in playing time.

This one component was the single biggest factor in my athletic success. Honestly, the reason training worked for me is because so few others apply it. I had a huge advantage simply because I practiced more. As an Athletic Director, I'm often the last to leave the campus and frequent our athletic facilities on nights and weekends. Less than 5% of our high school student-athletes put in extra work after team practices. Those who do are almost always producing fantastic results. Training works, apply it today!

Continue to Push

It may seem ironic that a chapter on avoiding burnout suggests pushing students harder! Yet, we must remember that people have a natural tendency to rise to meet given expectations. Humans crave direction, just look at the self-help aisle at your local bookstore, and direction is spurred by accountability.

Too many adults fail students by not holding them accountable. Providing feedback when students miss the mark encourages progress. When students are progressing it is difficult for burnout to arise. No doubt pushing students must be balanced, but it cannot be avoided or absent for engagement to occur.

Protect Confidence

Success produces confidence, however, constant harassment has the opposite effect. Downgrading remarks from adults and other students will produce negativity over time. There is absolutely a time and place to provide constructive feedback when the performance is below-par; however, every day is not the day!

Know that struggles will arise from time to time. However, having a process allows students to reap positives out of negative experiences. Trusting in that process allows parents and coaches to take on the proper perspective, even when desired results are not evident. Not only will students' confidence remain intact, but they will also develop resiliency despite failures.

Maintaining a calm outlook prevents students from burning out because of depression or discontent. Remember, the hook to athletics is the great feeling produced by making plays, winning games, and interacting with teammates. The endorphins produced from physical exertion enliven the body and produce a sense of accomplishment. These traits keep participants returning for more. Don't ruin the positivity with overwhelming negativity.

Confidence is often derailed due to fear. When students are constantly in fear, confidence will never bloom. Fear could be due to a demeaning coach, overwhelming level of play, or other circumstances. In any case, the results can be devastating.

While an initial fear of joining a new team or starting a new sport is natural, constant fear is not. This fear causes hesitation, discontent, and lack of joy. I've witnessed students with loads of talent, never display it, due to fear. As adults, we must subtract constant anxiety from athletic participation. Student mistakes are a healthy part of the process; do not retard growth by increasing the impact of each mistake.

PROS AND CONS OF MULTI-SPORT PARTICIPATION

Multi sport participation is not only a great way to avoid burnout, it's also awesome for building athleticism. While the final two to three years of high school are best spent focusing on one sport (two at most); prior to this time, switching up sports helps develop rarely used muscles and movements and builds new brain pathways. If learning one language is great, learning two is superb.

However, multi-sport can have its drawbacks. The key to becoming an Engaged Athlete is commitment evidenced by training. Multi-sport athletes are so busy that they often don't take the time to commit to a training schedule. Flippantly going between sports without taking either seriously will develop the opposite of commitment. Rather than creating Engaged Athletes, many are creating students who are 'Involved in Everything' (IE). IE Athletes often never maximize the takeaways which commitment provides. For example...

Multi-sport athletes often possess loads of natural athleticism that allows them to be successful in a variety of sports. The danger in a little organic success is that it develops the mentality that improvement is given and not earned. While I am a huge proponent of playing multiple sports before Sophomore year in high school; establishing commitment always takes priority no matter how many sports you choose.

As with any rule, exceptions always exist. Some students have the capacity to truly commit to multiple sports. Furthermore, some sports are great training partners for others (volleyball-basketball, football-wrestling, football-track, etc.). Still, those exceptions are not the norm so be sure you can commit to the process, not just the play.

Training also goes beyond skill development and includes body development. Multi-sport athletes generally go from one sport's season directly into another, leaving little time to develop strength and body mechanics for different movement patterns. At best this leads to performance inefficiencies, at worst, it leads to injury.

Whether you are on board with multi-sport participation or not multi-sport training is a great middle ground. Not only can it breathe new life into the training regimen, it also develops rarely used muscles and movement just as actually playing the sport does.

Soccer drills develop footwork skills that apply to all sports. Boxing develops shoulder and hand-eye speed. Football drills can help increase speed and explosion. Gymnastics is great for body orientation and physical strength, even in young boys!

CHAPTER 9

DEMYSTIFYING
THE COLLEGE CONUNDRUM

Receiving a free or discounted college education is one of the greatest opportunities available to students. As someone who has earned two undergraduate degrees and a Doctorate at no cost, I can testify to the power of this gift in my life.

To say receiving athletic aid has relieved me of a huge financial burden is an understatement. Having received over $300,000 in higher-educational expenses has been a tremendous blessing. Many graduates continue to pay for higher-ed degrees for ten to fifteen years after graduation. With the average cost of college tuition only expected to rise, athletics can be leveraged as a viable resource for helping cover college educational expenses and reducing financial stress for years to come.

Secondly, earning a college scholarship has provided a boost in life in the form of key character traits. Of the eight-million students participating in high school sports, only a half million will compete at NCAA schools. The process of juggling rigorous academic studies with arduous athletic training is a gauntlet that many will never face. Competing collegiately is one of life's rare challenges, (similar to Armed Forces training, Law school, or running a marathon) few people have the will or opportunity to experience. Surviving and thriving in this rare air creates confident and success-minded youth who become highly sought after.

Lastly, earning an athletic scholarship has transformed my connections. Investing blood, sweat and tears alongside others creates incredible human bonds. Traveling all over the world to play a game that entertains millions also creates bonds with those you may not even know. Suffice it to say, I have friends and fans in high places. These bonds have profoundly impacted me and have helped shape my life.

These and other great benefits are awaiting those who truly engage through athletic participation. Below are a few tips to guide those intent on helping students earn college scholarships.

Parents - Finance & Educate

Parents become so enamored with the thought of receiving free schooling that they mistakenly assume that the process is free as well. Parents will spend close to the amount of college tuition, between grade school and high school, just to place a student in a position to earn college funding.

Training, apparel, travel, equipment and other expenses will add up over time. But parents should view these costs as worthwhile investments in their student's future. Similar to stock market investing, diversification is key. Diversify your student's portfolio through actively investing in a variety of opportunities that will prepare your student for the collegiate ranks. After all, these investments can reap much higher rewards.

Ordering your budget to account for these costs will reduce the stress and the pressure to earn a college scholarship. While free options for team play and training do exist; cost will become a factor at some point (whether time or money) and you need to be prepared. Too many miss out on the transformational experience of collegiate athletics because the costs became a major hindrance or strain on the family's budget.

Parents should also educate themselves early on the various levels and opportunities available to college athletes. Prep schools, Junior Colleges, NAIA and NCAA Divisions II and III offer fantastic alternatives to the well-known NCAA DI level. As you become aware of the various options, you will become more confident in your student's ability to earn free or reduced educational expenses.

Performing this due diligence will allow you to become familiar with others who have reached the college level and learn about their path. As you learn, you will make connections which will provide further resources. Begin to dig the tunnel early, to provide a pathway to your goal.

Coaches - Communicate Progress

Sometimes the pressure to earn a scholarship is placed on coaches and can create awkward situations between students and coaches. This is because expectations often produce pressure which lead to a variety of unexplained emotions. Coaches typically respond by not accounting for the student's goals or feeling the need to make false promises.

Instead of making promises let's match the passion each student brings to the equation to accomplish their goals. Students who are passionate about becoming a college athlete will put in the energy, effort, and passion to do so. This passion should be matched by their coaches towards their goal. Students who are not as committed to their goal should accordingly be matched with less passion. This is not to suggest that coaches should care less for those whom aren't as passionate towards accomplishing their goal; but coaches should not want something more than the student does either. Ultimately, unequal passion will cause anxiety in either the coach or student, which lessens desire and breeds discontent.

This does not mean providing unearned positions or opportunities for students who want to play collegiately. However, it does mean communicating assessments often. Let's say Susan is not working hard or is developing bad practice or personal habits; both her and her parent should be made aware of how her actions negatively affect her ability to earn a scholarship. If Larry has just had a huge game or season which has attracted the eye of college programs; his coach should inform him of the best ways to leverage his momentum to receive more college offers. More over, if circumstances require Dan's role to be altered (more/less playing time, position change, etc.); notify him how fulfilling this new role will help him towards achieving his goal of becoming a college athlete.

Do not assume students and parents know everything about the process of earning a college scholarship. Many false assumptions lead to negativity. For example, many parents are unaware of collegiate academic requirements or the role club sports play in earning a scholarship.

Parents and students can more readily commit to the process when consistant feedback and education exists. Similar to marriage, we can expect commitment to a unified goal when we communicate according to a spouse's needs. Yet when students and parents do not receive feedback they become frustrated with the process and disconnected from their goal.

Simple conversations go a long way toward calming fears and anxiety that students and parents have when things do not manifest according to plan. These conversations can also provide much needed guidance, even when things are going well.

The mission of every educator is to prepare students for their next level, whether that means College, the Armed Forces, Technical School, or the workforce. No matter the destination, once a student has his sights set, matching the student's passion is the responsibility of those best positioned to help him reach the goal.

School Leaders - Make Information Readily Accessible

School leaders play a large role in producing an atmosphere of athletic engagement. Hiring high-level coaches and providing high-level resources (finances, facilities, equipment, etc.) play a huge role in student's awareness of athletics as an option for them.

Beyond this, school leaders should provide students with the critical information regarding the steps involved to get to their next level. Believe it or not this information is so hard to come by within schools. Instead, college and career readiness content should be prevelant across all campus departments.

It is no secret that many high school students gravitate to sports participation. Naturally, a large number of these participants will have interest in playing beyond high school. High-performing school districts will provide relevant information related to how students can make college athletics a reality. Administrators, counselors, and coaches can change a student's trajectory with this content. We as educators must recognize college athletic scholarships as a viable option rather than a shot at the lottery.

It was because of engaged coaches and counselors that I realized college athletics was an option for me. I'll never forget the day my coach brought me a stack of recruitment letters from local universities. I had no idea why or how these schools were sending me info! My coach set up a meeting between me and our counselor who explained the process. This simple conversation quickly let me know that I had options beyond high school. Consequently, my actions and accountability changed as I had hope in a great future!

Providing NCAA Clearinghouse details, college academic requirements, and local university contacts can get the journey to college started on the right foot. Also, connecting current students with former students who successfully earned college scholarships can provide key insight. Unfortunately, many students go their entire career without any knowledge related to becoming a college athlete. In the end, they are unprepared and ultimately unavailable to meet the requirements to go to the next level. Presenting this information in advance of recruiting sets the standards for students early.

Certain schools have become direct pipelines for college recruiters. These schools prepare students athletically, as well as, academically and provide the information which greases the wheels of the process. As a result, students and parents who prioritize earning a college scholarships seek out schools with this type of reputation. College coaches also seek out these schools because they know their students are prepared for college. This soon becomes a great area of marketing for the school and improves its athletic programs and school culture all because information was made available.

School Athletic Directors and Counselors must work together to prepare this information and make it readily available beginning as early as 6th grade. As students are awakened to the possibilities they will become curious, inspired, and many will begin to engage because of the content.

THE COLLEGE MYSTIQUE

It's a sad commentary, but many coaches skirt around the topic of college scholarships. However, a process of constant communication alleviates the unnecessary pressure and mystique surrounding collegiate athletics. Plenty of collegiate opportunities exist that make getting to college attainable for Engaged Athletes. I have witnessed students with less than one year of Varsity experience earn college offers. Yet, too many are overwhelmed by the often quoted probabilities of making it.

While it is true that only a small percentage of high school athletes go on to play in college, what popular statistics don't measure is the commitment-level of high school athletes. Only a small percentage are truly engaged. Students who become engaged (Train, Tribe, Tweak) automatically set themselves apart from others. More over, Engaged Athletes exponentially increase their odds at receiving a college scholarship.

Still, parents and students must also develop a confidence that a college scholarship is more reality rather than mere probability. When I ask many high level student-athletes what are their goals for playing the sport, most stammer and stutter about possibly playing at the next level. Very few have confidence that they can make it happen.

Receiving a college scholarship is a rare opportunity. It is not one that can be achieved half-heartedly. Students who fall short often lack confidence in knowing this is an achievable goal. Many look at earning a college scholarship as though it is as likely as making it to the pros!

Unfortunately, we often derail student confidence by shaming those who promote their desire to earn a scholarship. We create a mystique that causes anxiety and promotes doubt. Yet, with thousands of schools available, earning a college scholarship is not nearly as difficult as many make it. By committing to a process and applying unwavering faith toward the goal, free or reduced college expenses are a high possibility for any Engaged Athlete.

CONCLUSION

Education suffers without engagement. To get the most out of students, we must correctly use the resources which intrigue them. No doubt, athletics is a tool that captures the imaginations of young people and inspires them to be their best.

As with any tool, how it is used will determine its ultimate effectiveness. Half-hearted commitment levels from stakeholders deprive students of life-changing character, commitment, and collegiate opportunities. Instead, parents must thoroughly prepare students, coaches must prepare themselves, and schools must prepare their programs to make a difference.

Without a doubt, you have a role to play. Ask yourself, 'How am I using athletics to impact a student's life'? Students are even transformed by simply attending games. Those who become super fans, team managers, trainers, film crew, etc., come away motivated by being part of a something larger than themselves. Purpose is a heck of a thing!

Whether you are encouraging on the court improvement, or off the court excellence, engaging students through athletics is transformational.

What is my Why?

A student at my school, let's call him Henry, was a trouble-maker. Henry was constantly starting fights and being disruptive. Henry was disengaged in the classroom and would often find himself in the Principal's office for disturbing teachers and other students. As you can probably guess, Henry also has a terrible home life with no father, mother or siblings to speak of. Henry is being raised by an elderly grandmother, who cannot match his energy and has no idea how to inspire him.

Henry is a good basketball player, but at a school of our size, his skills were not quite good enough to make the team as a Freshman. When I met him at the start of his Sophomore year, he was known as a terror within the school. Without basketball, he was idle and lacked focus and purpose.

That same year, I had the opportunity to hire a new Golf Coach. Because our administrators and coaches had established our standards and mission as an Athletic Department, we were able to attract candidates that fit our focus. One of the important aspects of our culture is designing athletic programs that are attractive to students. As a result, the new golf coach re-designed the program in a manner that made it appeal to a different subset of students who had never considered it before.

Henry tried Golf for the first time since his Grand-father had introduced him to the sport, many years prior. He instantly became hooked! His skills improved week after week, and Henry finished his first season making the State Tournament as an alternate!

But it would take more for his character and be-havior to change. Throughout that first season, Henry was constantly in trouble due to bad be-havioral choices. We held weekly meetings with Henry to explain the behavioral expectations of our athletes. Henry reluctantly began to improve as a person, throughout his Junior year, but is-sues continued to occur. During the final two weeks of the season we suspended Henry from athletics for disruptive classroom behavior.

Henry finally saw the light. He realized the importance of Golf in his life and wanted to take advantage of all the opportunity it provided. It was at this point that Henry became an Engaged Athlete! His Senior year has been his best yet and he is on track to make State again and has attracted the eye of several junior college scouts.

You see many students, from various backgrounds (both good and bad) *participate* in athletics. But very few *engage*. Henry found purpose that drove his commitment level on the golf course and changed his life off the golf course. This is what Engaged Athletics is all about. Giving all students an enhanced educational experience through athletic engagement.

But it begins with commitment! Commitment from students; commitment from parents/guardians; commitment from schools; and, commitment from all administrators, to look deeper into athletics as an important educational tool that can be used to fully develop young people. Commitment enhances and changes lives.

For more great content (books, blogs, podcasts) and to connect with me go to Iamjasonlparker.com and subscribe today. Join the movement; Engage with us!"

RESOURCES

Coaching Coaches -
https://www.coaching-coaches.com/services

Instructional Coaching -
https://www.instructionalcoaching.com/

Game Changers -
https://www.gamechangerportal.com

National Interscholastic Athletic Administrators Association
- http://www.niaaa.org/

National Federation of State High Schools Associations-
http://www.nfhs.org/

Coach & A.D. -
https://coachad.com/

Boost Mental Toughness & Leadership -
https://www.aboostabove.com/

83013724R00076

Made in the USA
San Bernardino, CA
20 July 2018